SCHOLASTIC

# 10 MINUTE
# SATs TESTS
# MATHS

**AGES 10-11
YEAR 6**

# KS2

Scholastic Education, an imprint of Scholastic Ltd

Book End, Range Road, Witney, Oxfordshire, OX29 0YD

Registered office: Westfield Road, Southam, Warwickshire CV47 0RA

www.scholastic.co.uk

© 2017, Scholastic Ltd

1 2 3 4 5 6 7 8 9 7 8 9 0 1 2 3 4 5 6

British Library Cataloguing-in-Publication Data

A catalogue record for this book is available from the British Library.

**ISBN 9781407176109**

Printed by Ashford Colour Press

**Author**
Tim Handley

**Editorial team**
Audrey Stokes, Mary Nathan, Julia Roberts

**Series Design**
Scholastic Design Team: Nicolle Thomas and Neil Salt

**Design**
Claire Green and Scholastic Design Team: Neil Salt and Alice Duggan

**Cover Design**
Scholastic Design Team: Nicolle Thomas and Neil Salt

**Cover Illustration**
Adam Linley @ Beehive Illustration
Visual Generation @ Shutterstock

**Illustrations**
Adam Linley and Matt Ward @ Beehive Illustration

# Contents

# How to use this book

**10 MINUTE SATs TESTS**

**This book contains four different sets of maths tests for Year 6, each containing SATs-style questions. Each set comprises one arithmetic test and two reasoning tests, worth 28 marks in total. As a whole, the complete set of tests provides full coverage of the test framework for this age group, across the two strands of the maths curriculum: Number; and Measurement, geometry and statistics.**

Some questions require a selected response, for example where children choose the correct answer from several options. Other questions require a constructed response, where children work out and write down their own answer.

A mark scheme, skills check and progress chart are also included towards the end of this book.

## Completing the tests

- It is intended that children will take approximately ten minutes to complete each individual test; or approximately 30 minutes to complete each set of three tests.

- After your child has completed each set, mark the tests and together identify and practise any areas where your child is less confident. Ask them to complete the next set at a later date, when you feel they have had enough time to practise and improve.

**1.**      796 + 300 =

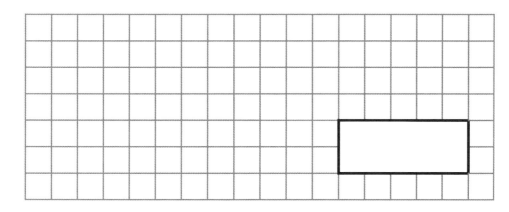

Marks

1

**2.**      4967 − 562 =

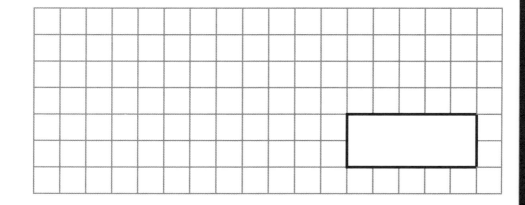

1

**3.**      ☐ × 9 = 72

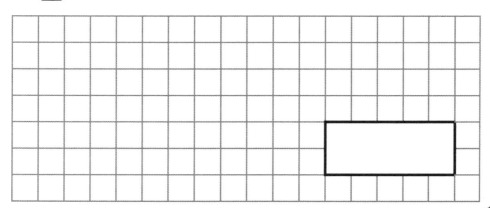

1

10
MINS

Marks

**4.** $10 + 4 \times 5 =$

1

**5.** $\dfrac{6}{8} - \dfrac{1}{4} =$

1

**6.** $1932 \div 100 =$

1

**7.** 45% of 880 =

1

**10 MINS**

**8.** 763.4 − 436.6 =

Marks

1

**9.** 56 × 8 =

1

**10.** 26 ⟌ 14,612

Show your method

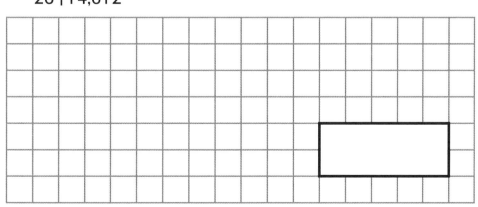

2

## Well done! END OF SET A TEST 1!

# Set A
## Test 2: Reasoning

10 MINS

Marks

**1.** Salma is making patterns out of shapes.

What will be the 14th shape in her pattern?

_____

1

**2.** Complete the table below. One has been done for you.

| Number | Rounded to the nearest 100 | Rounded to the nearest 1,000 |
|---|---|---|
| 385,552 | 385,600 | |
| 674,849 | | |
| 1,764,489 | | |

2

**10 MINS**

**3.** Maria says that $\frac{4}{5}$ is equivalent to $\frac{12}{15}$

Is she correct? Circle Yes or No.

**Yes  /  No**

Explain how you know.

_____

_____

_____

_____

_____

Marks

1

**4.** Use two of the digit cards below each time to make numbers that satisfy the statements below. You can only use each card once.

One has been done for you.

| 0 | 1 | 2 | 3 | 4 | 5 | 6 | 7 | 8 | 9 |

| 3 | 8 | is an even number. |
| 9 | | is a common multiple of 15 and 10. |
| | 7 | is a prime number. |
| | | is a square number. |
| | | is a cube number. |

2

9

**5.** The chart below shows how to convert between centimetres and inches.

Marks

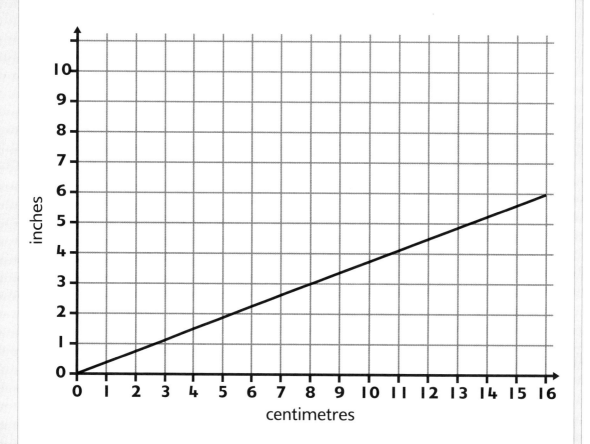

Approximately, how many inches is 13cm?  inches

 1

KEEP IT GOING!

10 MINS

**6.** The table below shows the weight of chocolate chips and flour that are needed to make different numbers of chocolate cupcakes.

Marks

Complete the table.

|  | 8 cupcakes | 16 cupcakes | 32 cupcakes |
|---|---|---|---|
| Chocolate chips | 50g | 100g | |
| Flour | 110g | | 440g |

2

Well done! END OF SET A TEST 2!

# Set A
## Test 3: Reasoning

**1.** Tick the diagrams below that show $\frac{3}{4}$

Marks

**a.**

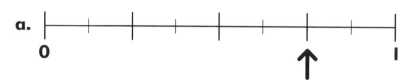

0                                      1

**b.**

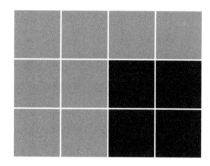

**c.**

**d.**

**e.**

1

**2.** Mark is programming a robot to follow a path from A to B.

Marks

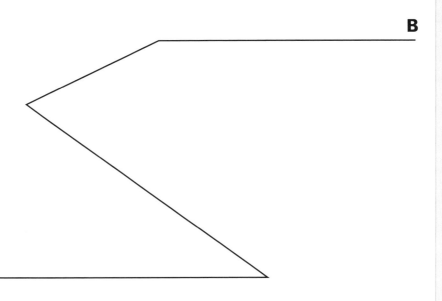

Drawn to scale

The robot travels in straight lines and can turn up to 360° clockwise or anticlockwise.

Mark writes the first instruction.

**Instruction 1:** Move forwards 10cm. Turn 145° anticlockwise.

Write the next three instructions.

**Instruction 2:** _____

**Instruction 3:** _____

**Instruction 4:** _____

2

**10 MINS**

**3.** Draw lines to match each fraction to its decimal equivalent.

Marks

$\frac{3}{4}$

0.46

$\frac{3}{8}$

0.75

$\frac{46}{100}$

0.25

$\frac{132}{200}$

0.375

$\frac{2}{8}$

0.66

KEEP IT GOING!

2

**Marks**

**4.** The Soft Toy Store had 30 standard-sized teddy bears in the sale and 20 extra-large bears. The price of an extra-large bear was £22 before the sale.

The shop has sold 30% of its stock of standard-sized bears.

How many standard-sized bears have they sold?

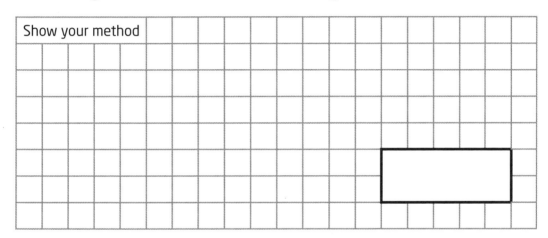

1

In the sale, the extra-large bears have a discount of 40%.
The shop sells all its extra-large bears in the sale.

How much money does the shop take for the extra-large bears?

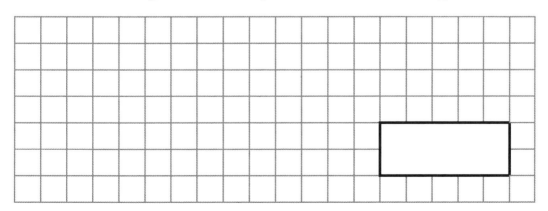

2

**Well done! END OF SET A TEST 3!**

# Set B
## Test 1: Arithmetic

 **10 MINS**

**Marks**

**1.** $141 \times 4 =$

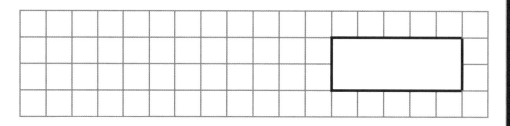

1

**2.** $1567 + 434 =$

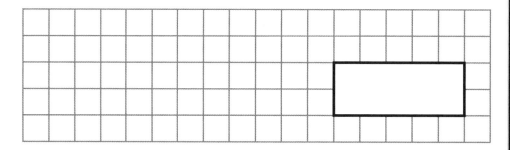

1

**3.** $7^2 =$

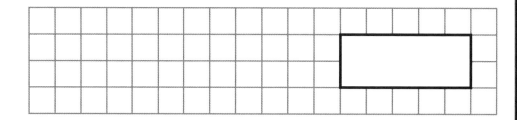

1

**4.** $3 \times 7 \times 3 =$

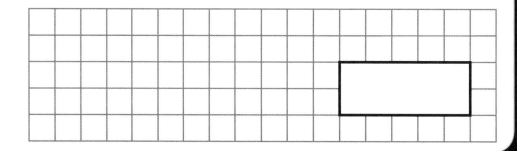

1

**5.** $\frac{3}{5} - \frac{2}{5} =$

Marks

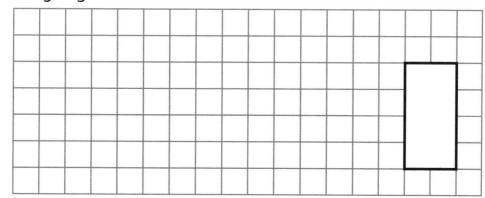

1

**6.** 3.56 × 1000 =

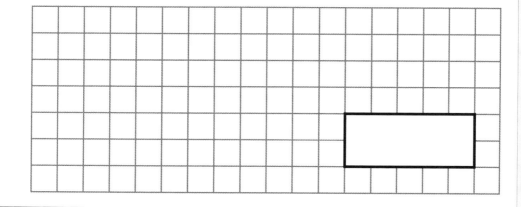

1

**7.** 30% of 1600 =

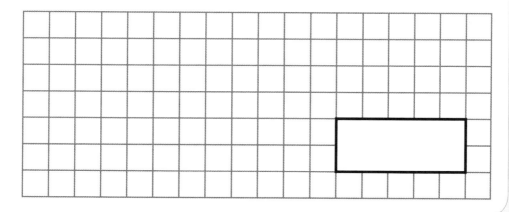

1

Marks

**8.**    5957 ÷ 7 =

1

**9.**

Show your method

$$\begin{array}{r} 6\ 7 \\ \times\ 2\ 3 \\ \hline \end{array}$$

2

**10.**    16.73 – 5.67 =

1

**Well done! END OF SET B TEST 1!**

# Set B
## Test 2: Reasoning

10 MINS

**Marks**

**1.** Order these measurements from smallest to largest.

1510mm      90cm      145cm      1.5m      910mm      1.05m

_____

1

**2.** The numbers in this sequence increase by 60 each time.

20      80      140      200...

The sequence continues in the same way.

Which number in the sequence will be closest to 600?

_____

1

KEEP IT GOING!

**3.** This diagram shows 2 rectangles on a coordinate grid.

The rectangles are identical.

Marks

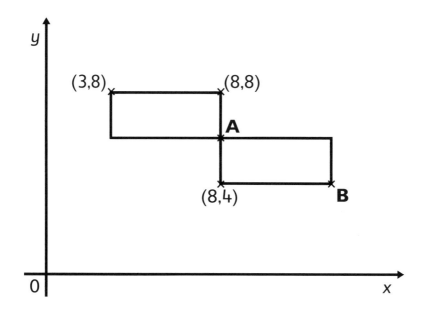

What are the coordinates of A and B?

A = _____

B = _____

2

10 MINS

**4.** A large chocolate bar has 16 squares.

Charlie eats $\frac{1}{4}$ of the bar and his sister eats $\frac{3}{8}$ of the bar.

How many squares of chocolate are left?

Marks

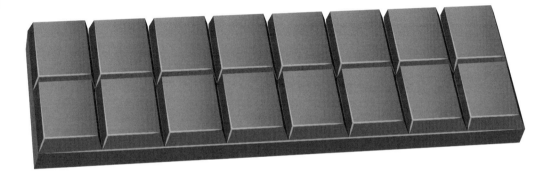

| Show your method | | | | | | | | | | | | | | | | | | |
|---|---|---|---|---|---|---|---|---|---|---|---|---|---|---|---|---|---|---|

2

**5.** Write the four missing digits to make this addition correct.

$$6 \,\square\, 3 \,\; 2$$
$$+ \; 2 \;\; 3 \;\; 3 \;\square$$
$$\overline{\;\square\; 1 \;\square\; 1\;}$$

2

21

**10 MINS**

Marks

**6.** Kieran says that $\frac{3}{4}$ is the same as 75%

Is he correct? Circle Yes or No.

**Yes / No**

Explain how you know.

_____

_____

_____

_____

_____

1

*Well done! END OF SET B TEST 2!*

# Set B
## Test 3: Reasoning

**1.** Tick the acute angles.

Marks

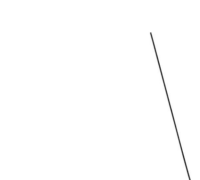

a) 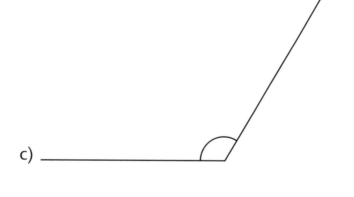   b)

1

c)

d)   e)

Use a protractor to measure the acute angles to the nearest degree. Write the size of the acute angles next to the diagrams.

1

Marks

**2.** Sandeep has attempted the calculation below.

$$78,543 + 3123 = 81,666$$

Explain how Sandeep could check his own answer.

_____

_____

_____

_____

_____

1

**3.** The table below shows the  average temperatures in Quebec City, Canada, throughout the year.

| Month | Jan | Feb | Mar | Apr | May | June | July | Aug | Sept | Oct | Nov | Dec |
|---|---|---|---|---|---|---|---|---|---|---|---|---|
| Temperature | −7° | −4° | 1° | 9° | 18° | 22° | 25° | 24° | 19° | 11° | 4° | −3° |

Which month is the coldest? _____

What is the temperature difference between the warmest and coldest months?

 °C

1

**10 MINS**

Marks

**4.** Place these fractions in order, starting with the smallest.

$\frac{1}{3}$      $\frac{9}{10}$      $\frac{6}{15}$      $\frac{1}{4}$      $\frac{6}{8}$

☐ ☐ ☐ ☐ ☐

1

**5.** A shop sells statues of Captain Hero.

Medium statues of Captain Hero are 20cm tall.

Large statues of Captain Hero are 1.75 times the height of a medium statue.

Not to scale.

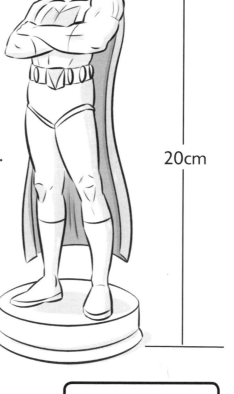

20cm

How tall is a large statue?

☐

1

25

**6.** A shop sells fruit.

Kain buys 3 apples and 1 banana.

He pays £1.10

Hope buys 6 apples and 1 banana.

She pays £1.70

How much does one apple cost?

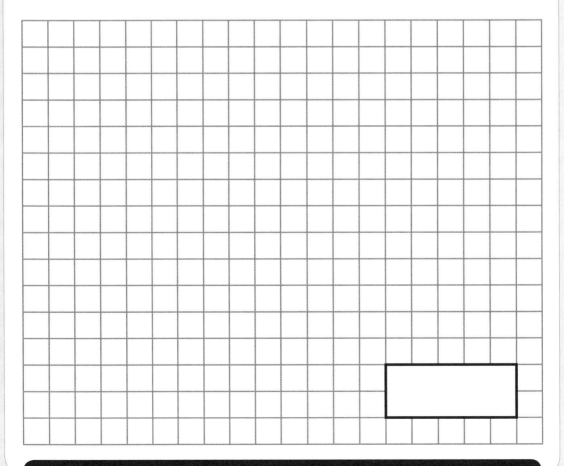

Marks

2

**Well done! END OF SET B TEST 3!**

# Set C
## Test 1: Arithmetic

10 MINS

**1.** 1011 – 300 =

Marks

1

**2.** 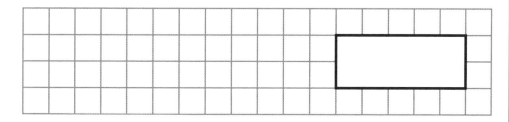 ÷ 9 = 1 2

1

**3.** 10 ÷ 2 + 3 × 6 =

1

**4.** $\frac{1}{3} \times \frac{2}{3} =$

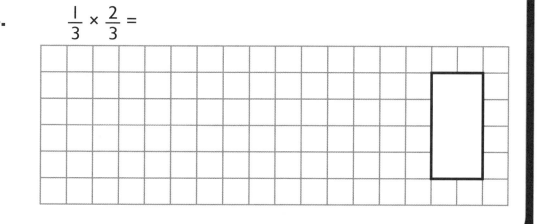

1

**5.**     $60,000 - 500 =$

Marks

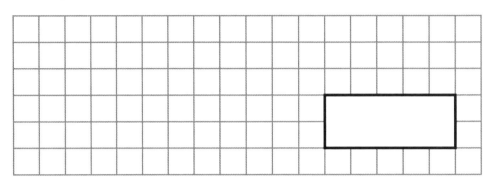

1

**6.**     45% of 120 =

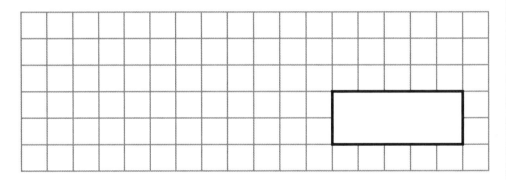

1

**7.**     $12^2 =$

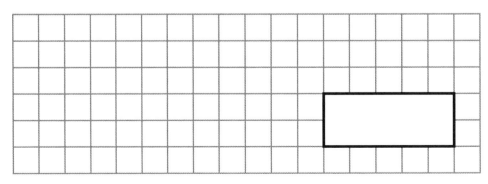

1

**10 MINS**

**8.** $65 \div 100 =$

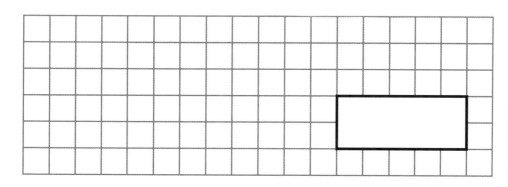

Marks

1

**9.** $94,322 + 13,498 =$

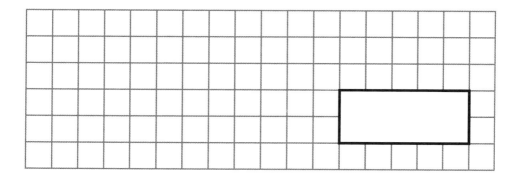

1

**10.**

Show your method

|   |   | 6 | 5 |
|---|---|---|---|
|   | × | 3 | 2 |

2

**Well done! END OF SET C TEST 1!**

# Set C
## Test 2: Reasoning

10 MINS

Marks

**1.** The timetable below shows the buses from Winchester to Romsey.

| 66 Winchester • Hursley • Woodley • Romsey | | | | | | |
|---|---|---|---|---|---|---|
| MONDAYS TO SATURDAYS | | | | | | |
| Winchester Bus Station | 1532 | 1622 | 1632 | 1712 | 1752 | 1907 |
| City Road | 1536 | 1627 | 1636 | 1717 | 1756 | 1910 |
| Royal Hants County Hospital | 1540 | 1632 | 1640 | 1722 | 1800 | 1914 |
| Hursley Post Office | 1555 | 1645 | 1650 | 1735 | 1810 | 1922 |
| Woodley Ashley Meadows | | | | | | |
| Cupernham Durban Close | | | | | | |
| Viney Avenue | 1605 | 1655 | 1700 | 1745 | 1820 | 1932 |
| Romsey Bus Station | 1610 | 1700 | 1705 | 1750 | 1825 | 1937 |

How long does the 1622 bus take to get from Winchester to Romsey?

 minutes

 1

Jordan lives near City Road. He wants to get to Viney Avenue for football practice at 5.30pm.

What time does he need to catch the bus from City Road?

_____

 1

Football practice lasts for 1 hour and 45 minutes. How many minutes will Jordan spend at Viney Avenue between getting off the bus to being picked up by his Mum straight after practice?

_____ minutes

 1

**2.** Look at the shapes below.

Marks

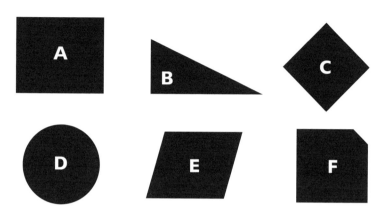

Write the letter of each shape in the correct place in this Venn diagram.

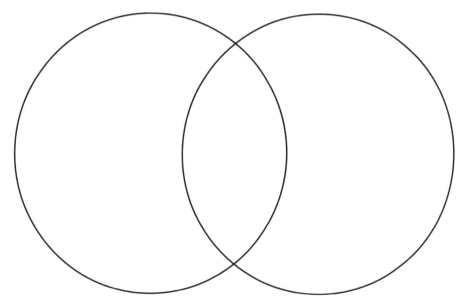

Has 2 or more
lines of symmetry

Has at least
one right angle

2

**10 MINS**

**3.** Write a number in each box below to make the calculations correct.

Marks

$$\boxed{\phantom{000}} \times 300 - 200 = 700$$

1

$$(100 - 20) + 50 \div \boxed{\phantom{000}} = 85$$

1

KEEP IT GOING!

**4.** $2x + 4y = 12$

$x$ and $y$ are positive whole numbers.

What are all the possible values of $x$ and $y$?

_____

_____

Marks

2

**Well done! END OF SET C TEST 2!**

# Set C

## Test 3: Reasoning

**1.** Olivia has drawn part of the net for a triangular prism.

Complete her net below.

Marks

1

**10 MINS**

**2.** Mary shares half of a large cake between herself and 3 friends.

Marks

What fraction of the whole cake does each person get?

1

___

**3.** Order these, starting with the **largest**.

$\frac{2}{8}$      0.81      $\frac{3}{4}$      80%      $\frac{1}{2}$      0.375

1

**10 MINS**

**4.**

Marks

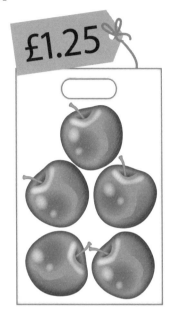

£1.25

£1.36

32p

A bag of 5 apples costs £1.25

A bag of 4 pears cost £1.36

A satsuma costs 32p

How much more does 1 pear cost than 1 apple?

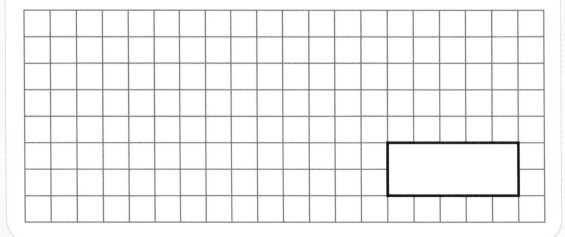

2

**10 MINS**

**5.** Meerkats at Open Zoo need 36m² of space inside their enclosure.

Their enclosure is a rectangle, and each side is a whole number of metres.

Complete some possible combinations of lengths and widths that their enclosure could have.

Marks

| Width | Length |
|---|---|
|  | 18m |
| 3m |  |
|  | 9m |
| 6m |  |
|  | 4m |

2

**6.** To make 500ml of pink paint, you mix 300ml of red paint with 200ml of white paint.

What is the ratio of red paint to white paint? Give your answer in its simplest form.

1

**Well done! END OF SET C TEST 3!**

# Set D
## Test 1: Arithmetic

**Marks**

**1.**     876 + 100 =

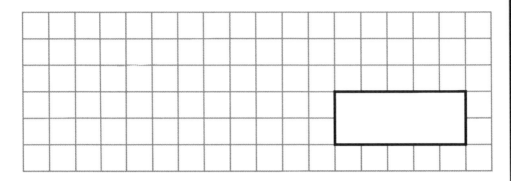

1

**2.**     8763 – 632 =

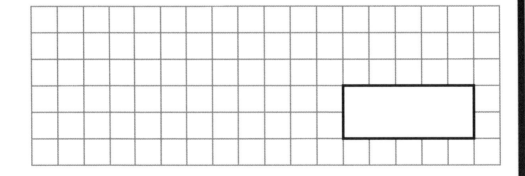

1

**3.**     60 × [          ] = 360

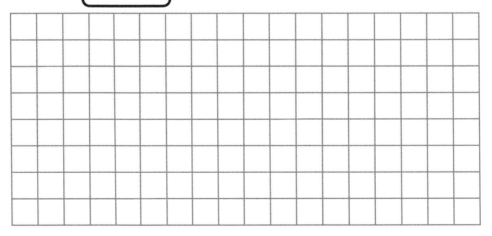

1

# Set D
Test 1: Arithmetic

Marks

**4.** $60 - 5 \times 2 + 1 =$

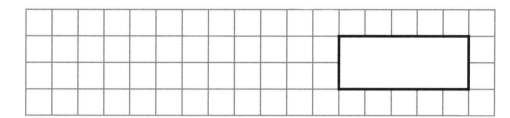

1

**5.** $\frac{3}{4} \times 3 =$

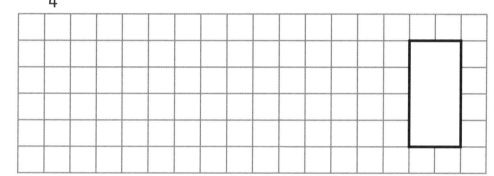

1

**6.** $7654 \div 100 =$

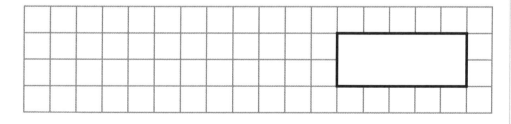

1

**7.** $81 \div 9 =$

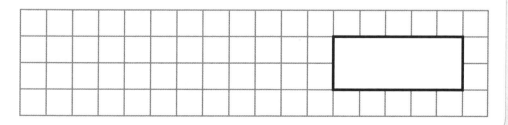

1

**8.**     867.6 + 496.6 =

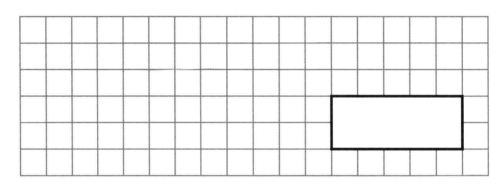

Marks

1

**9.**     87 × 6 =

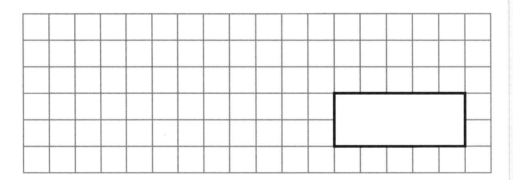

1

**10.**

Show your method

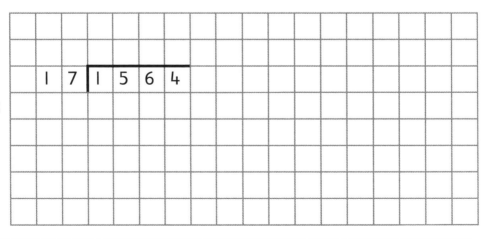

1 7 | 1 5 6 4

2

**Well done! END OF SET D TEST 1!**

Marks

**1.** Mary-Ann has 8 coins in her purse.

She has £1.65 in total in her purse.

What coins could Mary-Ann have in her purse?

_____

1

**2.** Save-a-lot supermarket buys cans of cola in packs of 24.

In the delivery today, they have received 12 packs.

How many cans of fizzy cola did they receive today?

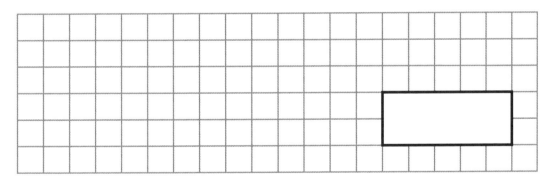

1

**10 MINS**

**3.** Martin eats 40% of a 120g bag of chocolate.

Siam eats 75% of a 55g packet of chocolate.

Rajan eats 55% of a 80g bar of chocolate.

Who has eaten the most chocolate?

Marks

_____

1

**4.** The graph below shows how the population of Greater London has changed over time.

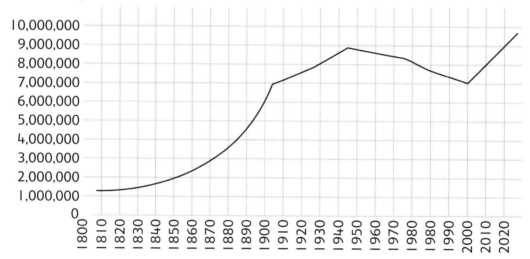

What year did the population of Greater London reach 6 million people?

_____

1

What was the increase in population between 2000 and 2010?

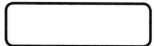

1

**5.** In a bag, the ratio of yellow balls to red balls is 1:3

There are 15 red balls.

How many yellow balls are there?

yellow balls

Marks

1

---

**6.** Nisha has a cuboid. Its sides are 2cm, 3cm and 5cm long.

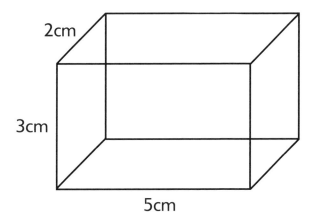

Not to scale

What is the volume of Nisha's cuboid? Use the correct units.

1

KEEP IT GOING!

**7.** $\frac{3}{5}$ of a class are boys.

There are 14 girls in the class.

How many children are in the class all together?

Marks

| Show your method |
|---|

children

2

Well done! END OF SET D TEST 2!

**1.** Write the correct sign between each statement below. Use the signs **<**, **=** and **>**.

One has been done for you.

| | | |
|---|:---:|---|
| 5400 ÷ 100 | **=** | 5.4 × 10 |
| 54 × 10 | | 540 ÷ 10 |
| 540 ÷ 100 | | 5.4 × 10 |
| 5.4 ÷ 10 | | 0.54 × 100 |
| 0.54 × 10 | | 540 ÷ 1000 |

Marks

2

**10 MINS**

**2.** The table below shows the population of the 7 largest cities in the UK in 2010.

Marks

| Cities, towns & districts | Population |
|---|---|
| London | 7,074,265 |
| Bradford | 483,422 |
| Glasgow | 616,430 |
| Sheffield | 530,375 |
| Birmingham | 1,020,589 |
| Leeds | 726,939 |
| Liverpool | 467,995 |

Which of these cities has the fewest people?

_____

Which cities have a zero in the hundred-thousands place?

_____

1

KEEP IT GOING!

**3.** Shade more squares so that $\frac{2}{5}$ of each diagram below is shaded.

Marks

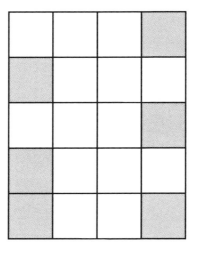

1

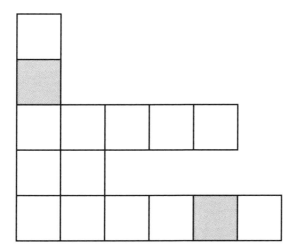

1

**4.** $3s + 12 = 24$

What is the value of $s$?

Marks

1

---

**5.** Dawn has collected money for charity every week for 6 weeks. She has recorded the amount she has collected in the table below.

| Week 1 | Week 2 | Week 3 | Week 4 | Week 5 | Week 6 |
|--------|--------|--------|--------|--------|--------|
| £36 | £40 | £18 | £52 | £67 | |

The mean amount she collected each week was £50.

How much money did she collect in Week 6?

Show your method

2

**Well done! END OF SET D TEST 3!**

# Notes

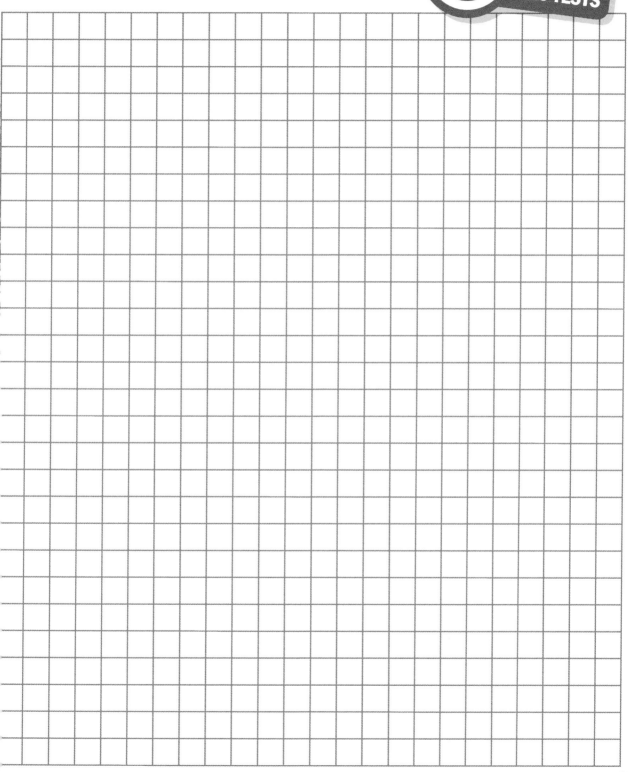

# Notes

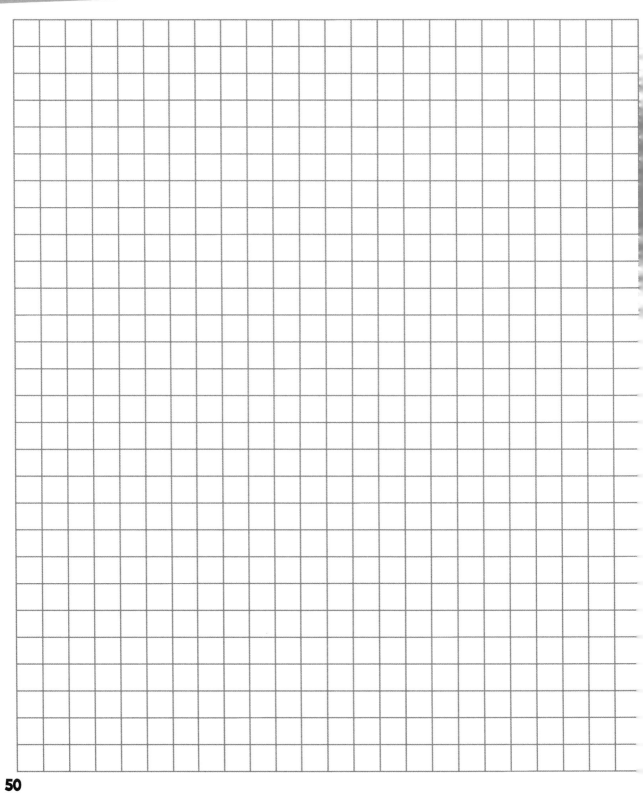

# Notes

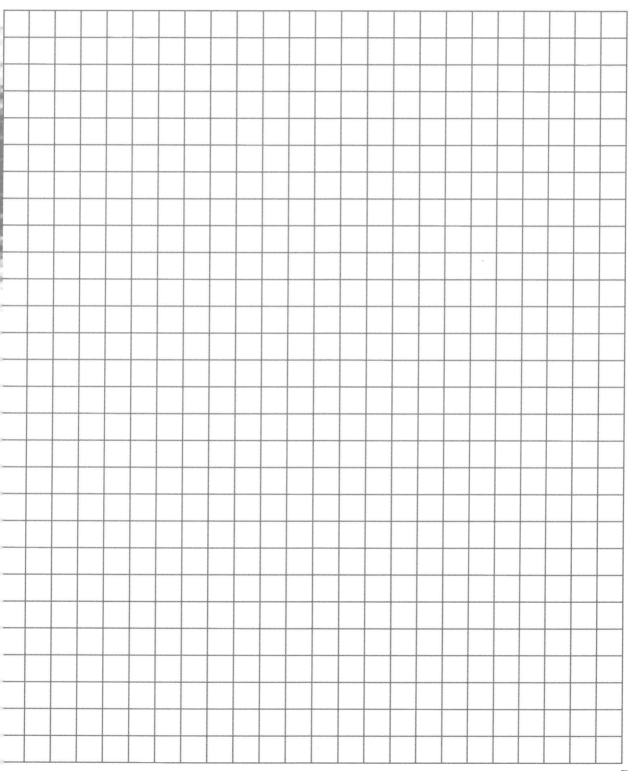

# Notes

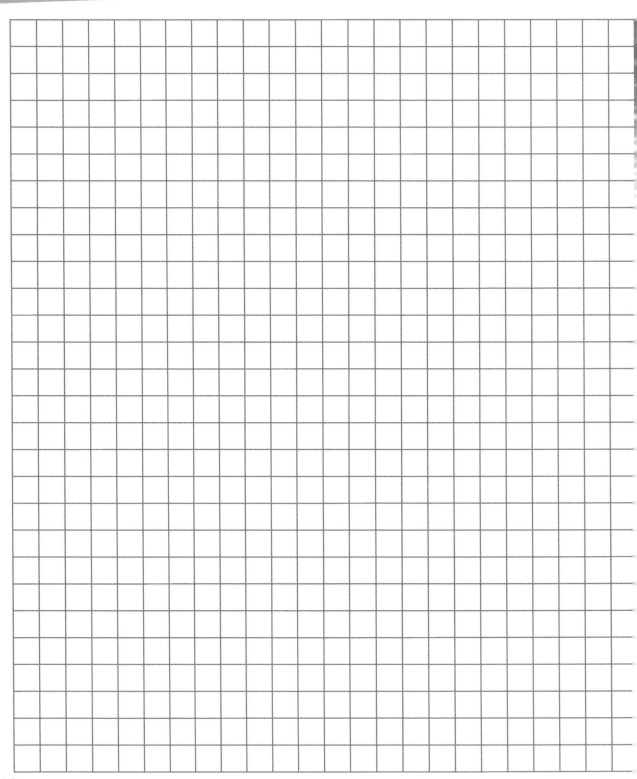

# Answers

Maths

| Q | Mark scheme for Set A Test 1 – Arithmetic | Marks |
|---|---|---|
| 1 | 1,096 | 1 |
| 2 | 4,405 | 1 |
| 3 | 8 | 1 |
| 4 | 30 | 1 |
| 5 | $\frac{1}{2}$ or $\frac{4}{8}$ or $\frac{2}{4}$ | 1 |
| 6 | 19.32 | 1 |
| 7 | 396 | 1 |
| 8 | 326.8 | 1 |
| 9 | 448 | 1 |
| 10 | 562<br>**Award 1 mark** for the formal written method for long division but with one arithmetical error.<br>Do not award any marks if no final answer has been written in the calculation. | 2 |

**Total**    **11**

| Q | Mark scheme for Set A Test 2 – Reasoning | Marks |
|---|---|---|
| 1 | Either the word **triangle** or a drawing of the equilateral triangle in the sequence. | 1 |

**2**

| Number | Rounded to the nearest 100 | Rounded to the nearest 1,000 |
|---|---|---|
| 385,552 | 385,600 | 386,000 |
| 674,849 | 674,800 | 675,000 |
| 1,764,489 | 1,764,500 | 1,764,000 |

**Award 2 marks** for all five correct.
**Award 1 mark** for three or four correct.

**2**

**3**

Yes
**Award 1 mark** for
- any answer which includes reference to the numerator and denominator being linked by the same scale factor, eg 'Because 4 × 3 is 12 and 5 × 3 is 15' OR
- any answer which lists all equivalent fractions to $\frac{4}{5}$ until $\frac{12}{15}$ is reached, if it is accompanied by an explanation, eg 'We know because some equivalent fractions to $\frac{4}{5}$ are $\frac{4}{5}$, $\frac{8}{10}$, $\frac{12}{15}$, $\frac{16}{20}$ – the numerator increases by 4 each time and the denominator by 5 each time. $\frac{4}{5}$, $\frac{12}{15}$ is in this pattern.' OR
- any answer which shows the equivalence pictorially.

**1**

**4**

90 is a common multiple of 15 and 10
17 is a prime number
25 is a square number
64 is a cube number
**Award 2 marks** for all four correct.
**Award 1 mark** for three correct.
Do not give credit for answers which contain digits that have been repeated.

**2**

| 5 | **Award 1 mark** for an answer in the range 4.8–5.2 inches inclusive. | 1 |

|  | | 8 cupcakes | 16 cupcakes | 32 cupcakes |
| --- | --- | --- | --- | --- |
| **6** | Chocolate chips | 50g | 100g | **200g** |
|  | Flour | 110g | **220g** | 440g |

**Award 2 marks** for both answers correct.
**Award 1 mark** for one correct.

Total 9

| Q | Mark scheme for Set A Test 3 – Reasoning | Marks |
| --- | --- | --- |

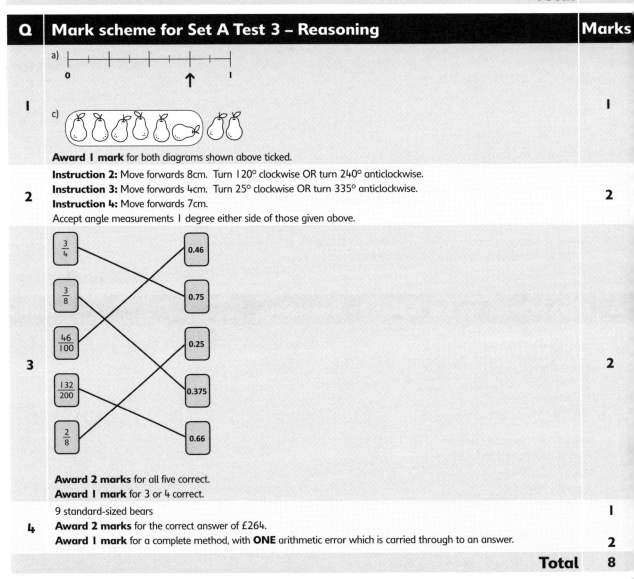

**1**

a) (number line with arrow)

c) (pears diagram)

**1**

**Award 1 mark** for both diagrams shown above ticked.

**2**

**Instruction 2:** Move forwards 8cm.  Turn 120° clockwise OR turn 240° anticlockwise.
**Instruction 3:** Move forwards 4cm.  Turn 25° clockwise OR turn 335° anticlockwise.
**Instruction 4:** Move forwards 7cm.
Accept angle measurements 1 degree either side of those given above.

**2**

**3**

$\frac{3}{4}$ — 0.46
$\frac{3}{8}$ — 0.75
$\frac{46}{100}$ — 0.25
$\frac{132}{200}$ — 0.375
$\frac{2}{8}$ — 0.66

**2**

**Award 2 marks** for all five correct.
**Award 1 mark** for 3 or 4 correct.

**4**

9 standard-sized bears

**1**

**Award 2 marks** for the correct answer of £264.
**Award 1 mark** for a complete method, with **ONE** arithmetic error which is carried through to an answer.

**2**

Total 8

| Q | Mark scheme for Set B Test 1 – Arithmetic | Marks |
| --- | --- | --- |
| 1 | 564 | 1 |
| 2 | 2,001 | 1 |
| 3 | 49 | 1 |
| 4 | 63 | 1 |
| 5 | $\frac{1}{5}$ | 1 |
| 6 | 3,560 | 1 |

| 7 | 480 | 1 |
|---|-----|---|
| 8 | 851 | 1 |
| 9 | 1,541<br>**Award 1 mark** for the formal written method for long multiplication but with one arithmetical error.<br>Do not award any marks if there is an error in the place value of the multiplication or if no final answer has been written in the calculation. | 2 |
| 10 | 11.06 | 1 |
|  | **Total** | **11** |

| Q | Mark scheme for Set B Test 2 – Reasoning | Marks |
|---|------------------------------------------|-------|
| 1 | 90cm    910mm   1.05m   145cm   1.5m   1,510mm | 1 |
| 2 | 620 | 1 |
| 3 | A = (8,6)<br>B = (13,4)<br>**Award 1 mark** for each correct answer.<br>DO NOT accept transposition of coordinates, eg A = (6,8) is incorrect. | 2 |
| 4 | 6 squares<br>**Award 2 marks** for the correct answer of 6 squares.<br>**Award 1 mark** for evidence of appropriate working, but with one error allowed in the addition or subtraction of fractions only, eg<br>$\frac{1}{4} + \frac{3}{8} = \frac{2}{8} + \frac{3}{8}$ = WRONG ANSWER   eaten.<br>This would then need to be carried through to an answer to receive the 1 mark. | 2 |
| 5 | 6 [8] 3 2<br>+ 2 3 3 [9]<br>[9] 1 [7] 1<br>**Award 2 marks** for all four digits correct.<br>**Award 1 mark** for three digits correct. | 2 |
| 6 | **Award 1 mark** for an explanation that calculates $\frac{3}{4}$ and 75% of the same number, proving they are equal, eg $\frac{3}{4}$ of 100 = 75,  75% of 100 = 75<br>or shows $\frac{3}{4}$ as a fraction over 100, eg $\frac{3}{4} = \frac{?}{100}$  4 × 25 = 100, 3 × 25 = 75, and therefore, $\frac{3}{4} = \frac{75}{100}$ and $\frac{75}{100}$ = 75% | 1 |
|  | **Total** | **9** |

| Q | Mark scheme for Set B Test 3 – Reasoning | Marks |
|---|------------------------------------------|-------|
| 1 | **Award 1 mark** for angles a, b and d ticked.<br>**Award 1 mark** for the correct measurements of the acute angles, within the ranges given:<br>a: 43°–47° inclusive<br>b: 70°–76° inclusive<br>d: 13°–17° inclusive | 1<br>1 |
| 2 | **Award 1 mark** for answers that show that Sandeep could either:<br>• use an estimation to check his answer, eg Sandeep could round the numbers to 78,500 and 3,100, which when added together equal 81,600 – this is close to his answer, so he is probably correct.<br>• use the inverse to check his answer, eg Sandeep could use the inverse: he could calculate 81,666 – 3,123, and if this equals 78,543, he will know he is correct. | 1 |
| 3 | January<br>32°C | 1 |
| 4 | $\frac{1}{4}$    $\frac{1}{3}$    $\frac{6}{15}$    $\frac{6}{8}$    $\frac{9}{10}$ | 1 |
| 5 | 35cm | 1 |

20p or £0.20

**6**

**Award 2 marks** for the correct answer of 1 apple costs 20p   or £0.20

If the answer is incorrect, award 1 mark for evidence of appropriate working, eg

£1.70 – £1.10 = £0.60

£0.60 ÷ 3 = wrong answer

**Accept for 1 mark** £20 OR £20p OR 0.20p as evidence of appropriate working.

Working must be carried through to reach an answer for the award of 1 mark.

**2**

| | | **Total** | **8** |
|---|---|---|---|

| Q | Mark scheme for Set C Test 1 – Arithmetic | Marks |
|---|---|---|
| 1 | 711 | 1 |
| 2 | 108 | 1 |
| 3 | 23 | 1 |
| 4 | $\frac{2}{9}$ | 1 |
| 5 | 59,500 | 1 |
| 6 | 54 | 1 |
| 7 | 144 | 1 |
| 8 | 0.65 | 1 |
| 9 | 107,820 | 1 |
| 10 | 2080 <br><br> **Award 1 mark** for the formal written method for long multiplication but with one arithmetical error. <br> Do not award any marks if there is an error in the place value of the multiplication or if no final answer has been written in the calculation. | 2 |

| | | **Total** | **11** |
|---|---|---|---|

| Q | Mark scheme for Set C Test 2 – Reasoning | Marks |
|---|---|---|
| 1 | 38 minutes | 1 |
| | 1636 (allow 16.36 or 4.36pm) | 1 |
| | 135 minutes (He gets off the bus at 1700 and practice ends at 1915.) | 1 |

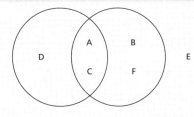

Has 2 or more       Has at least one
lines of symmetry      right angle

**2**                   **2**

**Award 2 marks** for all five letters correctly placed.

**Award 1 mark** for four letters correctly placed.

Award no marks where letters have been added to the Venn diagram in more than one place.

| 3 | **3** × 300 – 200 = 700 | 1 |
|---|---|---|
| | (100 – 20) + 50 ÷ **10** = 85 | 1 |

$x = 2$ and $y = 2$
$x = 4 =$ and $y = 1$

**4**

**Award 2 marks** for both answers correct.
**Award 1 mark** for one correct answer with no incorrect answers.
**Award 1 mark** for both correct answers with no more than one incorrect answer.

**2**

| | |
|---|---|
| **Total** | **9** |

| Q | Mark scheme for Set C Test 3 – Reasoning | Marks |
|---|---|---|

**1**

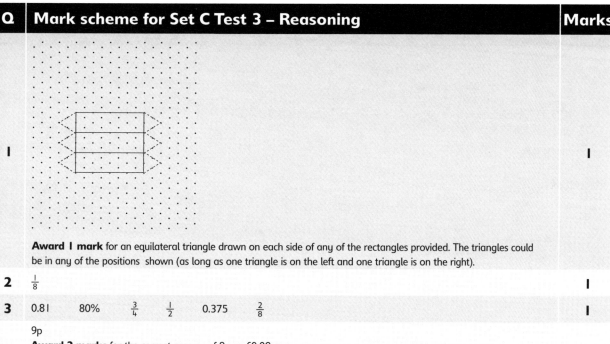

**Award 1 mark** for an equilateral triangle drawn on each side of any of the rectangles provided. The triangles could be in any of the positions shown (as long as one triangle is on the left and one triangle is on the right).

**1**

**2** $\frac{1}{8}$

**1**

**3** 0.81    80%    $\frac{3}{4}$    $\frac{1}{2}$    0.375    $\frac{2}{8}$

**1**

**4**

9p
**Award 2 marks** for the correct answer of 9p or £0.09
**Award 1 mark** for evidence of appropriate working, eg
£1.25 ÷ 5 = £0.25
£1.36 ÷ 4 = WRONG ANSWER
Wrong answer – £0.25 = answer given.
**For 1 mark**, working must be carried through to an answer.

**2**

**5**

| Width | Length |
|---|---|
| **2m** | 18m |
| 3m | **12m** |
| **4m** | 9m |
| 6m | **6m** |
| **9m** | 4m |

**2**

**6** 3:2

**1**

| | |
|---|---|
| **Total** | **8** |

| Q | Mark scheme for Set D Test 1 – Arithmetic | Marks |
|---|---|---|
| 1 | 976 | 1 |
| 2 | 8,131 | 1 |
| 3 | 6 | 1 |
| 4 | 51 | 1 |
| 5 | $2\frac{1}{4}$ or $\frac{9}{4}$ | 1 |
| 6 | 76.54 | 1 |

| Q | | Marks |
|---|---|---|
| 7 | 9 | 1 |
| 8 | 1,364.2 | 1 |
| 9 | 522 | 1 |
| 10 | 92<br>**Award 1 mark** for the formal written method for long division but with one arithmetical error.<br>Do not award any marks if no final answer has been written in the calculation. | 2 |
| | **Total** | 11 |

| Q | Mark scheme for Set D Test 2 – Reasoning | Marks |
|---|---|---|
| 1 | Several possibilities, eg<br>£1    20p    20p    10p    10p    2p    2p    1p<br>£1    20p    20p    20p    2p    1p    1p    1p<br>50p    50p    50p    10p    2p    1p    1p    1p<br>Accept any order, or any other clear indication. | 1 |
| 2 | 288 | 1 |
| 3 | Martin (48g) | 1 |
| 4 | 1900<br>1 million | 1<br>1 |
| 5 | 5 | 1 |
| 6 | 30cm³<br>Correct units must be shown for the award of the mark. | 1 |
| 7 | 35 children<br>**Award 2 marks** for the correct answer of 35.<br>**Award 1 mark** for evidence of appropriate marking which is carried through to an answer, eg<br>$1 - \frac{3}{5} = \frac{2}{5}$<br>$\frac{2}{5}$ of the class are girls.<br>$\frac{1}{5}$ of the class = WRONG ANSWER.<br>WRONG ANSWER × 5 = answer given. | 2 |
| | **Total** | 9 |

| Q | Mark scheme for Set D Test 3 – Reasoning | Marks |
|---|---|---|
| 1 | 54 × 10 **>** 540 ÷ 10<br>540 ÷ 100 **<** 5.4 × 10<br>5.4 ÷ 10 **<** 0.54 × 100<br>0.54 × 10 **>** 540 ÷ 1,000<br>**Award 2 marks** for all four correct.<br>**Award 1 mark** for three correct. | 2 |
| 2 | Liverpool<br>London and Birmingham (all answers required for 1 mark) | 1 |
| 3 | 2 additional squares shaded<br>4 additional squares shaded | 1<br>1 |
| 4 | s = 4 | 1 |
| 5 | £87<br>**Award 2 marks** for the correct answer of £87<br>**Award 1 mark** for evidence of the full correct method, with 1 arithmetic error, eg<br>50 × 6 = 300<br>36 + 40 + 18 + 52 + 67 = 213<br>300 – 213 = WRONG ANSWER | 2 |
| | **Total** | 8 |

General notes for parents and teachers:

- In the National Curriculum tests, approximately 85% of marks are from the Place Value, Addition and Subtraction, Multiplication and Division, Fractions, Ratio and proportion and Algebra content areas.

- Where a statement below indicates that the skill should be completed mentally, rough jottings are acceptable.

## Number – number and place value

I can read, write, order and compare numbers up to 10,000,000 and say what each digit is worth, eg what is the digit 8 worth in 8,321,566?

I can round any whole number, or decimal with up to three decimal places, to a required degree of accuracy, eg round 43.813 to the nearest whole number.

I can use negative numbers both in and out of context, and calculate differences across zero, eg what is the difference between –9 and 18?

## Number – addition and subtraction

I can use my knowledge of the order of operations (BODMAS) to carry out calculations involving the four operations, eg explain why $3 + 6 \times 5$ is 33, not 45.

I can add multiples of 10, 100 and 1000 **mentally**, eg 7400 + 3100 = ?

I can add two digit numbers **mentally**, eg 46 + 65 = ?

I can add any number to a multiple of 10, 100 or 1000 **mentally**, eg 5600 + 438 = ?

I can use and explain the formal written method for addition, including of decimals, eg

```
    5 2 9 2
 +  3 8 9 6
    9 1 8 8
```

I can use and explain the formal written method for subtraction, including of decimals, eg

```
    5 7 6 3 1
 -    4 5 9 3
    5 3 0 3 8
```

I can solve addition and subtraction multi-step problems in context, deciding which operations and methods to use and why, eg Kian and Hope both collect football stickers. Hope has 8 more stickers than Kian. Together they have 40 stickers. How many stickers does each child have?

## Number – multiplication and division

I can **mentally** multiply and divide whole numbers and decimals by 10, 100 and 1000, eg 56.3 ÷ 100 = ?

I can **mentally** multiply any number between 1–12 by another number between 1–12, eg 7 × 12 = ?

I can **mentally** use the related division facts for the 1–12 times tables, eg 132 ÷ 12 = ?

I can **mentally** multiply multiples of 10 together, eg 80 × 90 = ?

I can **mentally** multiply numbers with 1 decimal place by a whole number, eg 0.7 × 8 = ?

I can **mentally** multiply any number by 0 and 1, eg 87,654 × 0 = ?

I can **mentally** double and halve any number with up to three digits, eg double 67 = ?

I can **mentally** multiply any two digit number by a single-digit number, eg 34 × 6 = ?

I can multiply numbers with up to 5 digits by a one-digit number, using a formal written method, eg

```
    8 7 3 2
×         6
_____

```

I can multiply numbers with up to 4 digits by a two-digit whole number, using a formal written method, eg

```
    5 6 7 8
×       3 1
_____

```

I can divide numbers with up to 4 digits by a single-digit whole number, using a formal written method of division,

and show any remainders as whole number remainders, fractions, or by rounding, as appropriate for the context,

eg $8\overline{)7\ 4\ 3\ 5}$

I can divide numbers with up to 4 digits by a two-digit whole number, using the formal written method of long division, and show any remainders as whole number remainders, fractions, or by rounding, as appropriate for the context,

eg $3\ 2\overline{)8\ 7\ 6}$

I can give my answers using written division methods to 2 decimal places, eg 654 ÷ 7 = ? Give your answer to two decimal places.

I can identify prime numbers up to 100, eg I can list the first 8 prime numbers.

I can identify and work out square and cube numbers, eg I can list the first 3 cube numbers.

I can identify factors and multiples, including common factors and common multiples, eg what are the common factors of 24 and 18?

I can solve problems involving addition, subtraction, multiplication and division, eg Kieron and Isaac go to the shop. Kieron buys 3 packets of biscuits for 56p each and a bottle of fizzy drink for £1.32. Isaac buys 4 packets of the same biscuits, and a large packet of crisps for 95p. How much more money does Isaac spend than Kieron?

# Skills check

Maths

## Number – fractions (including decimals and percentages)

I can find equivalent fractions for any given fraction, eg list four equivalent fractions for $\frac{3}{7}$.

I can simplify fractions by using common multiples, eg express $\frac{6}{8}$ in its simplest form.

I can compare and order fractions, including fractions which are greater than 1, eg order $\frac{4}{5}$, $\frac{1}{3}$, $\frac{8}{3}$ and $1\frac{1}{3}$.

I can convert between mixed numbers and improper fractions, eg express $\frac{8}{3}$ as a mixed number.

I can add and subtract fractions with different denominators, including mixed numbers, eg $\frac{7}{8} + 1\frac{1}{4} = ?$

I can multiply pairs of proper fractions, writing the answer in its simplest form, eg $\frac{1}{3} \times \frac{1}{2} = \frac{1}{6}$.

I can divide proper fractions by whole numbers, eg $\frac{3}{4} \div 2 = \frac{3}{8}$.

I can calculate decimal equivalents for simple fractions, eg what is $\frac{3}{8}$ as a decimal?

I can express any decimal as a fraction, eg what is 0.68 as a fraction?

I can recall and use equivalences between simple fractions, decimals and percentages, eg what is $\frac{2}{3}$ expressed as a percentage and as a decimal?

## Ratio and proportion

I can solve problems involving the calculation of percentages, eg what is 55% of £1.40?

I can use ratios in simple contexts, eg the ratio of red paint to white paint is 1:3. If Kian used 750ml of white paint, how much red paint does he use?

I can solve problems involving similar shapes where the scale factor is known or can be found, eg scale this shape by a scale factor of 1.5.

## Algebra

I can use simple formulae, eg the retail cost of a bag of crisps in Kieron's Convenience shop is expressed as 2c + 10p where c = the cost price of the crisps. How much would the retail price of the crisps be if the cost price was 25p?

I can generate and describe linear number sequences, eg describe the rule for this number sequence 7, 13, 19, 25... what will the tenth number in this sequence be?

I can express missing number problems algebraically, eg the amount of sugar used in doughnuts is $\frac{1}{3}$ the mass of the doughnut. Write a formula to calculate the amount of sugar needed for any mass of doughnut.

I can find pairs of numbers that satisfy an algebraic equation with two unknowns and find all possibilities, eg what could x and y be in 3x + 2y = 16?

# Skills check
Maths

## Measurement

I can solve problems involving the calculation and conversion of units of measure, using decimal numbers up to three decimal places in my answer where appropriate, eg 60kg + 1331g = ?

I can calculate the area and perimeter of rectangles (including squares) using a formula, eg what is the area and perimeter of a square with side lengths 6cm?

I can calculate the area of triangles using a formula, eg what is the area of a triangle with a base length of 8cm and a height of 6cm?

I can calculate the area of parallelograms using a formula, eg what is the area of a parallelogram with a base of 10cm and a height of 6cm?

I can calculate, estimate and compare volume of cubes and cuboids using standard units, eg what is the volume of a cuboid with the dimensions 4cm × 5cm × 2cm?

## Geometry

I can draw 2D shapes using given dimensions and angles, eg draw a triangle which includes an angle of 75° and a side length of 10cm.

I can recognise, describe and build simple 3D shapes, including making nets, eg draw 3 possible nets for a cube.

I can find unknown angles in any triangle, quadrilateral, regular polygon and around a point, eg if a quadrilateral has angles of 60°, 70° and 104°, what is the size of the fourth angle?

I can name parts of a circle, including radius, diameter and circumference, and know that the diameter is twice the radius, eg draw a circle and label the radius, diameter and circumference.

I can identify perpendicular and parallel lines, eg I can identify which lines are parallel and perpendicular in a rectangle.

I can describe and mark on positions on a four quadrant coordinate grid, eg plot (−5,5).

I can draw and translate shapes and reflect them in the axes, eg translate this shape by 1 unit horizontally and 4 units vertically.

## Statistics

I can interpret graphs and charts, including pie charts and line graphs, and answer questions based on them, eg look at this line graph. What was the highest temperature reached during the day?

I can calculate and interpret the mean, eg the mean of a set of four different numbers is 10. What could the numbers be?

# Progress Chart

Fill in your score in the table below to see how well you've done.

| | Score |
|---|---|
| Set A Test 1 | |
| Set A Test 2 | |
| Set A Test 3 | |
| Set B Test 1 | |
| Set B Test 2 | |
| Set B Test 3 | |
| Set C Test 1 | |
| Set C Test 2 | |
| Set C Test 3 | |
| Set D Test 1 | |
| Set D Test 2 | |
| Set D Test 3 | |
| **TOTAL** | |

| Mark | |
|---|---|
| **0–38** | Good try! You need more practice in some topics – ask an adult to help you. |
| **39–79** | You're doing really well. Ask for extra help for any topics you found tricky. |
| **80–112** | You're a 10-Minute SATs Test maths star – good work! |

GREAT WORK!

Well done!

You have completed all of the 10-Minute SATs Tests

Name: _____

Date: _____

# QUICK TESTS FOR SATs SUCCESS

## BOOST YOUR CHILD'S CONFIDENCE WITH 10-MINUTE SATs TESTS

- Bite-size mini SATs tests which take just 10 minutes to complete
- Covers key National Test topics
- Full answers and progress chart provided to track improvement
- Available for Years 2 and 6

**Find out more at www.scholastic.co.uk**